for &

Goo

departn...

of nghts,

but,

Comet over Greens Norton

Si me

Aug '13

COMET OVER GREENS NORTON:
NEW AND SELECTED POEMS

SIMON CURTIS

Shoestring Press

Printed by imprintdigital
Upton Pyne, Exeter
www.imprintdigital.net

Typeset by narrator
www.narrator.me.uk
enquiries@narrator.me.uk

Published by Shoestring Press
19 Devonshire Avenue, Beeston, Nottingham, NG9 1BS
(0115) 925 1827
www.shoestringpress.co.uk

First published 2013
© Copyright: Simon Curtis

The moral right of the author has been asserted.

ISBN 978 1 907356 81 0

ACKNOWLEDGEMENTS

Grateful acknowledgments to the following magazines and newspapers, where some of the poems first appeared: *Acumen, Assent, The Australian, The Charles Lamb Society Bulletin, Critical Quarterly, Critical Survey, The Dark Horse, Dorset Yearbook, Encounter, The Independent, The Interpreter's House, London Magazine, London Review of Books, New Welsh Review, Other Poetry, Poetry Durham, Poetry Nottingham, Quadrant* (Australia), *The Spectator, The Thomas Hardy Journal, The Times Literary Supplement, Verse*.

Bookplate by Ian Stephens RE, reproduced with thanks to the artist.

Some of the poems were published in the following collections: *On the Abthorpe Road* (Davis Poynter, 1975), *Mrs Paine* (NW Arts chapbook, 1979), *Faber Introduction 6* (1985), *Sports Extra* (Littlewood, 1988), *Views: Northamptonshire Poems* with wood-engravings by Ian Stephens RE (Northampton, 1990), *The Chronometer* (Paper Bark Press, Sydney chapbook, 1990), *Twenty Sonnets and a Coda* (Poet and Printer chapbook, 1993) and *Spike Island Spring* (Shoestring Press chapbook, 1996).

'Satie at the End of Term' appeared in the *New Oxford Book of Light Verse* and the *Penguin Book of Light Verse*; 'Dorchester Pastoral' (now retitled 'Dorchester Rural') in *Speaking English, Poems for John Lucas*; and 'Gym' was commended in the Bridlington Philip Larkin Poetry Competition.

Thanks to Alan Munton for his support.

FOR CAROLE

I think the groundhog'd like to chew
A fresh-baked saffron bun from Looe
Or, even better, two.
– Email to Maine

CONTENTS

New Poems

THREE SCORE AND TEN

The Parkinson's mild shake
Affecting my left hand
Is good for nothing, really,
Save that I have found

When beating eggs for omelettes
The odd left tremble's fine,
Agile, fast and practical,
An upside to decline?

AT WEMBURY

For Beth Levinsky

Cirl buntings skulking deep in cliff-top gorse –
See there, you point, *below that clump of pine*:
Reduced in all to just five hundred pairs,
Once common birds, they're now in steep decline.

With stubble ploughed for winter cereals
And crop sprays wiping foodsource insects out,
Intensive farming's land-use changes mean
These scrubland margins map their last redoubt.

My first cirl bunting field-glass sighting, too,
This south-west coastal path damp afternoon;
The silhouetted pine, the cliff-top gorse,
And song-notes, hear, that could go silent soon.

SPINSTER AND PUSH-BIKE

*...the old maids biking to Holy Communion through
the mists of autumn mornings...
(George Orwell in "England Your England")*

Why does the spinster George Orwell conceived,
 Pedalling to church through autumnal mist,
 Strike such a chord as image and presence,
And so anachronistically persist?
You see her referred to, time and again,
As a kind of symbol of Englishness –
 Doughty and dogged, one of the old school?
Or lonely old maid, shy as a mouse?

 Landscape in autumn, singleton figure
And Holy Communion merge to evoke
A live and let live England your England –
The "mild knobbly faces" of tolerant folk.
O would it were so and could be believed,
With spinster and push-bike Orwell conceived.

ARMS PARK '72

We decided on impulse that we'd drive
From Manchester two hundred miles
To Cardiff Arms Park to watch Barry John
Play for the last time for Wales,

And be there to see the famous Welsh team
Take on France (they'd Villepreux) that year,
With Mervyn Davies, the Pontypool front three,
Gareth Edwards and JPR.

We started at dawn on a damp March day
For the four hundred mile round trip;
I recall how it was – thirty years young –
And the freedom, the fellowship.

FINANCIAL PAGES

"Excessive liquidity" I read. And fret.
 Share prices floating on huge seas of debt,
 With inflation, they say, once again a threat.

Are my savings and pension all that secure,
What with hedge funds and buy-out consortia
And private equity partnerships galore?

Then credit default swaps and CDOs –
Collaterised debt obligations (those) –
And futures markets and leverage, who knows?

I shouldn't fret, they say. I ought to trust
That corporate fundamentals are robust,
And the commodities market won't turn to bust.

So that's all right, *pro tem*. Or appears to be.
It's what asset management involves, I see.
What price old virtues, thrift, good husbandry?

KURT SCHWITTERS IN AMBLESIDE

A thousand miles (and how much more in taste?)
From art's apostasy in Hanover
Where Dada anarchy fired your youth, is
The green slate gable, blue-stone guest house air
Of Ambleside, its streets austere, sedate.
You lived your last years here, obliged, for cash,
To paint the local burghers. They, you said,
"Don't like to see the brush-strokes". What a clash!

At first, the finished portraits hung here seem
Conventional. But look at them close-to:
Dark skeins, odd blues and eerie whites, sharp fleck
And scumble-whorl – the fire! The restless drive!
The young man's eye, compelling, still shines through.
Old burgher heads, but so distinct, alive!

BROTHER'S ROOM

I push the door that guards your room.

The handle's spring is still too loose.
The window's deep embrasure, still,
Ensures a quiet, familiar gloom.
It's warm, inside, to stuffiness,
As always, and here beneath my shoe
The same ill-fitting oak plank creaks.
The cistern snuffles as before,
And there, in the far top corner, too,
Are the bruises from forgotten leaks.

As before, as before, and all
Seems tranquil here, unchanged, a berth
Time's not made obsolete, for how
Metallic still, the old clock ticks;
The corner cupboard, crammed with kit,
Must smell of dubbin still, and earth,
And liniment, the same . . . and talk
Of how The Saints* lined up last week
At Franklins for the Leicester game,
With Jeeps back, White and Butterfield,
Burns in my ears once more –
                          Save now
There is a snapshot here, that's new,
Framed in glass and *passe-partout*,
By the sea-shell on the mantelpiece:
Your young Joanna eyes the room
From in front of a stuccoed house
In Ireland, somewhere, far. My niece,
Who reminds you, when here now, of home.

* *The Saints – Northampton R.F.C. – play at Franklin's Gardens, a local Mecca.*

Devil Among the Tailors (2011)

COMET OVER GREENS NORTON

Binoculars focusing true
   (Ten o'clock from Cassiopeia),
I pick out Hale-Bopp – head, coma and tail –
   Its sky-smudge icicle-clear,

Remote over Allibone's farm
   On its orbit hurtling away,
And due to return from the depths of space
   In four thousand years, so they say;

As far ahead as Homer is back,
   Two million calendar days.
To focus true on time-scales like that
   Unnerves to the quick as I gaze,

Stood at midnight on Blakesley Hill
   In the frost by a neighbour's fence.
What on earth will Hale-Bopp look down on,
   Four millennia hence?

CARPE DIEM

Place Aristide-Briand, Thonon

In memory of Julian Pianta-Snelling

Mathieu climbs into the mauve spaceship,
Gripping the steering-wheel tight;
As the roundabout starts to go round,
He's brought into and then out of sight.

At a café table, we're sat close by
And wave each time he appears;
Tunes the roundabout's sound-system plays
Are out-of-date by fifty years,

Post-World War Two accordion stuff –
That's back to our childhood, we laugh.
Crouched in his cockpit, the boy doesn't care
(Well, he's only three and a half);

Entirely engrossed in his own here-and-now,
He shows how to seize the day
To us *loco parentis* sixty-year-olds
In a pretty exemplary way.

SNOW GEESE

Snow geese came into view like a kept promise
– William Fiennes

It wasn't the image of snow geese
Way up in the blue Dakota sky
Migrating north toward Canada
His words sparked off in my inner eye,

But more what his simile implied
Of a preordained scheme of things:
Snow geese in Vs, like a promise kept,
With a following wind at their wings,

Where man is one with nature and part
Of some higher determining law –
Set free from self-doubt's self-questionings –
Inevitable, driven and sure.

PASTORAL

A yellow JCB
Is flailing hedgerows bare
On the road by Kingthorn Mill.
Hoarse revving sours the air

As wood is skived raw white
In a slashing wholesale rip
Of this September's store
Of blackberry, rose-hip,

Haw, elder, honeysuckle
And pale blue early sloes;
The cost-effective way
That husbandry now goes.

No joke to see the scathe
Of this familiar lane
I've known for forty years –
Though flailers, raising Cain

To standardise each hedge
With teeth of tempered steel,
Make clear to pastoralists
What farm work is for real.

WINTER FLOWERING

Planted by previous owners,
And entirely new to me,
It's a kind of amaryllis –
Nerine bowdenii –

Which, programmed by its DNA,
Must bloom from bulb or corm
Into midwinter British murk
And not midsummer warm;

'Spidery icing-sugar-pink'
The gardening handbook says;
Perverse and girly and forlorn
In raw east wind like today's.

THE HARRISON-KENDALL CHRONOMETER (K1)

'Our never-failing guide' Cook called it –
The brilliant Kendall chronometer;
For with Greenwich time fixed for three long years,
He knew what he owed the inventor:

Those longitude bearings, essential to chart
A voyage that would alter the earth,
As in oceans unmapped as outer space,
Untested but true, K1 kept faith.

Science it was, then, followed the flag,
With the urge to know and discover
Flowing natural as the Pacific tides
Astern of the Bark *Endeavour*;

So if, from some dead ground, poet,
You mark Carina or Southern Cross
As emblems of sense of estrangement,
Of human littleness or loss,

Then consider the fixed Meridian,
Chronometer, sextant and stars;
Think how what's measurable may offer
Its own propitious metaphors,

Like the gravity-pull of Reason –
Wherein readings from light-points provide
Facts for the skilled to work on and chart,
For those who may follow, a guide.

A FEW SUPERLATIVES

The Mersey valley starts at Cheadle Heath,
Where steep streets climb and, timeworn, terrace-rows
Clad primal rock with brick, and at whose foot
The dirtiest river in all Europe flows.

Our city likes to boast superlatives:
The biggest campus; football team the best;
Slum clearance tops; new shopping mall A1;
Add in the Mersey, then. The dirtiest.

We've humour, though, to compensate for all
That chemical and acid toxin stew;
Pollution there so dire, our river rates
Fire-hazard listing – in that rarest, too.

I walked there on a wet-through day last week;
Two horses browsed a dingy urban lea
Near pylon and dead willowherb and gorse –
Their chestnut coats as rich as rich could be.

CRUNCH

I try to fathom how it works:
How risk's secured via packaged debt,
A form of asset traders trade
Through SIV and CDO.
And then there are derivatives,
Which sound like supercharged roulette,
Options and futures – place your bet.
What point in thrift, frugality,
In long-term savings, meant to grow,
When money's cheap and interest low,
With credit's Big Bang go, go, go?

Ask analysts at Citigroup,
Ask Bank of England, ask the Fed,
Do market fundamentals still
Comprise a culture you can trust?
What happens, say, when loans fall due?
If Wall Street trading screens turn red
Alarming days could lie ahead.
I try to fathom how it works –
Short-selling, hedge-funds and the rest –
Then hear the breaking news (you've guessed)
As, one by one, the banks go bust;

Bear Stearns and Lehman, B & B,
Glitnir and Fortis, Northern Rock ...
Words like freefall, meltdown, slump,
Mean balance-sheets all shot to hell.
Ask laissez-faire free marketeers
Why Alan Greenspan, taking stock,
Expressed his disbelief and shock?
I try to fathom how it's turned
To fuck-up on a whopping scale –
Deregulation's Holy Grail
A grand illusion. Verdict: fail.

NORTH AND HILLARD

Lay siege (that's *obsidere*); make a breach;
Or man the walls and barricade the gate;
In serried ranks, let cohort troops lay waste
And cause great slaughter as they subjugate ...

In North and Hillard's true blue *Latin Prose,*
Across a gap of nearly five decades,
I re-read sentences I struggled with
For Common Entrance, then O level grades;

Bellum administrare and so on,
And grammar rules which seemed immutable –
No daily life, no childhood, schooldays, love,
Decidedly no poetry at all.

How could they have approved of Horace, who
Had flung away his shield at Philippi?
Then, amnestied, lived on his Sabine farm
To write with tolerant urbanity

Of country life, of sane, realistic hopes –
And girls and friendship and Caecuban wine –
Both wary of imperial politics
And all too well aware of fleeting time.

And what he wrote endured two thousand years,
That shrewd, ironic and Horatian tone,
Which (oh my education!) I was forced
To seek out and discover on my own.

FOINAVON

That great day when at Aintree
   Foinavon came in first –
the National also-ran,
   the dud, the hopeless case –
while the crowd, astonished, gaped,
   and all the punters cursed,
we knew that for once we'd seen
   a miracle taking place;

you double bézique, sheer fluke,
   you royal flush, blind luck,
you treble chance come right,
   you pawn who took the queen,
you Cinderella tale,
   you swan once ugly duck,
five-hundred-to-one wild guess,
   and black renegade thirteen;

you bullion found in the attic,
   you legacy hope come true,
you hit, you hole-in-one,
   you random long shot star,
what worlds of incredible chance
   will find their mark in you –
Foinavon, galloping home,
   when things that we dreamt of, are.

SNAP

In the snap I took of you
At Little Moreton Hall,
You looked extremely brassed off,
Worn down, it seems, by it all;

Hand from the wheelchair arm-rest
Upraised as for form's sake,
In a glum salute on this,
Our special May Day break;

Grasping your ice-cream cone
(A double, raisin and rum)
As, son and carer, I coax
'Let's have a photo, Mum!'

Neither the old, eccentric,
Endearingly lop-sided
Half-timbered, moated house –
Which should have delighted –

Nor the solicitous guides
Could really help at all
That damp grey May Day noon
To raise our joint morale.

We each knew perfectly well
How we'd tried our level best;
Let's drive back to the Home,
You said, even that, and rest.

IN ST FIMBARRUS CHURCH, FOWEY

In memoriam VMSC

This was (so says a small brass plate)
Sir Arthur Quiller-Couch's seat;

Anthologist and novelist
And Lloyd George party loyalist,

Yacht Club Commodore and Mayor,
Who held the Cambridge English Chair.

*

I've come in for a moment's break,
Reflection and remembrance sake,

To kneel to say a prayer for you,
Close to that staunch old liberal's pew;

(His *Oxford Book of English Verse*
A well-known text to you, of course –

An Eng Lit undergraduate
In long-gone 1928).

And how you would have chuckled, too,
To think of Quiller-Couch – of 'Q';

Your laughter, I remember that,
As I begin. *Requiescat.*

GYM

A *thud thud thud* of running on the spot,
As trainers pound out dogged treadmill miles;
Below the gym's steel air-conditioning ducts,
We focus on vague distance. No one smiles.

My heart-rate read-out reads red one-one-six –
Ten minutes pounding gone, ten more to go;
A fifty-something woman in gold specs
Slides on a cable-rower to and fro.

In what looks like a virtual Tour de France,
Two youths, head down, pump legs on bike-machines;
A chap with sideburns flexes dumbbell flies;
A girl does fitball squats in cut-down jeans.

A bank of TV screens, the volume off,
Relays some golf, a chat show and the news;
Adductors, hamstrings, triceps, biceps, pecs –
We pay the health-gods' sweaty work-out dues,

And exercise just like automatons,
Our faces glum, oh fit to bust a gut,
As men think six-pack abs and women dream
Of slimmer hips and shapely bust and butt.

Get bio-rhythms right, boost self-esteem,
That fitter, leaner, greener goal in view;
This England; work-life balance and less stress –
Heart-rate in red's now up to one-four-two.

MECHANICAL NIGHT CLUB BRONCO

They say girls ride it topless some nights, too.
Well, they deserve a medal, that's my view;

Just picture it – . Try not to, then. At all.
Cold shower. Cross-country run. Miss Greer. St Paul.

An atavistic British LCM
Where male gaze stalks. One should, of course, condemn.

But she agreed to it, you can't deny ...
They made her. She's a victim ... Don't see why;

It's the world and its fancy (not its wife) ...
It's bad ... It could be worse. It's Freud. It's life.

These things go on, so take them in good part?
It's hard to focus once the broncoes start.

CANAL, HIGH LANE

What warmed, I suppose, was the *thought* of heat –
Touched randomly off by the coaly fumes
Which blew my way on a bitter east wind
As I stood near a lock, numb to the bones –

A narrow-boat passing, crunching through ice
(*Lark* on its cabin in curlicued gold),
Whose chimney's black smoke for an instant seemed,
By a trick of sense, to abate the cold.

The sour tang worked its perceptual sleight,
If not quite a world from a grain of sand,
Then warmth out of freeze, improbably real –
Mind over matter, or the other way round.

A schedule to keep, the *Lark* passed from sight.
Cracked ice, as it settled, glittered with light.

AT BELLINGHAM

Out from the peat-brown waters,
Mayflies are starting to hatch,
Eddying wing-beat blurs of white
The fresh cross-breezes catch,

Causing the pale twilight specks
To appear to drift and dither,
As they couple, conceive and, spent,
Fall back to reeds or river.

Primeval forms, the mayflies teem,
Renewed once again into flight
Like flakes in a flurry of snow,
Bizarre in June half-light –

Leaving the two of us torn
Between enchantment and grief;
Thrilled by their epiphany,
Aware, though, just how brief

These lives, so soon effaced;
Such beauty and such waste.

GIFT

A fiver each for the children;
A small 'dab in the fist', I say –
Using a phrase you used to use
Which, now that you've passed away,

Takes on a new significance,
Like something by chance left behind.
How your clear-cut inflexion of voice
Comes vividly back to mind.

CLICHÉ

'It's not the end of the world', I said
To the check-out girl as I paid,
On finding out that my loyalty card
Was not in my wallet, mislaid.

The old cliché I used with a shrug
Might have been better thought through,
The morning after the one that had been
The end of the world for you.

PROM

It's Constant Lambert's *Rio Grande,*
Live tonight from the Albert Hall;
A piece you loved but for me fresh ground;
I switch on my new digital –

The first Proms season since you died,
And, irony, your birthday date;
As the players start to hit their stride,
I listen like a surrogate.

SEAFRONT CAFÉ BAR

On the terrace, an elderly couple
Sit wordless at coffee together,
With apparently nothing on earth
That they want to say to each other.

There's a widower, too, with his paper
(And crossword for something to do)
With lots he would like to talk over,
But no one to tell it all to.

FACE VALUE

The seaside rough sleepers, three of them, move
On a shine of sand in clear silhouette –
Their bags and bedrolls left in a heap
On foreshore shingle above tideline wet –

Competing at skimming stones out to sea,
Joshing together and making high fives,
As carefree as kids, or a seeming so,
To take at face-value three glimpsed lives.

PRODUCER THEATRE

Enter Autolycus, wheeling a Vespa;
She'd a punk hair-do, was wearing a parka,

And spoke Glaswegian Scots, to boot.
The audience thought it all a great hoot.

Innovative, bold, whatever you will –
But what space was left for *acting* to fill?

PHOTOGRAPH OF THE ARTIST

Anag-rhyme poem

Seeing him so, stiff as a ramrod,
Glaring and bearded, who would demur
With such a gruff bank-manager?
Oh sure, his regimen
Is facts, curt speech, plain words; for see
How man-to-man the straight eye is.
A stickler for the system, yes ...

But look below: the caption says Matisse.

Though expectations lead you on
You cannot tell from looks, oh no.
This ramrod man was colour's lover;
With what light heart he'd joy and revel
In frank large shapes and sensuous line;
How finely his bright nudes stretch or kneel.

Our automatic labels
The photograph belies.
Intent on the outward, we may well lose
The nature of the artist's soul.

Mark what a midget Keats was, under five foot.
And Byron at one time was a sixteen stone tough.

SATIE AT THE END OF TERM

The mind's eye aches from Henry James,
Like arms from heavy cases, lugged for miles.
    Theme and structure, imagery and tone.

From Lawrence, too; how hard I dug
For insights sunk, yards deep, in turgid prose.
    Theme and structure, imagery and tone.

Web of necessity in *Daniel Deronda*,
Gloom in *Dorrit*, gloom in Flaubert,
One more week to go, at
    Theme and structure, imagery and tone.

So fitful-fresh as April sun,
You're welcome, clown;
Your good melodic dissonance
Will pierce low clouds of syllabus
    With humour's grace,
    Mercy of irreverence.

DARKLING THRUSH – BOCC*

An amber alert's been announced on behalf
    Of various species of bird,
And it includes the storm-cock mistle thrush,
    The fellow that Hardy once heard.

It's not so un-Hardy-like, too, to reflect
    As New Year's glasses are clinked,
That some ninety-nine years since he penned his piece,
    His mistle might soon be extinct.

Though when the song's gone, we'll conjure it up
    On CD or the internet;
In a technical way, we'll be able to cope –
    Log on and tune into it yet,

As an echo, like virtual hope.

*Birds of Conservation Concern

THE GLEBE

For Andy and Fi

Our moon-cast shadows slither as we climb
Across the chill white glebe toward the house.
Like icy jewels, yet moving, ceaseless, look!
You point the Pleiades, then Sirius.

Through ground set harling-hard, the Quair swirls on;
Trout in its freezing flow, alert still, mark
Vibrations from our boots at thirty feet,
And flick in fright from deep to deeper dark,

The dog sixth-senses movement we can't see.
And stops, ears pricked. Who's there? Who's watching? Stares?
A qui vive earth – apart, on edge, all nerves –
Stakes out what we call ours, the trespassers.

EGG

I could hear a youth in the passing car
Guffaw with his mates as he chucked the egg,
Fantastically funny, oh ha ha ha,
When it hit me, *splat*, knee-high on the leg.
My cords sticky-smeared with wet from the yolk,
I'd become, on my way to the pub that night,
The butt of some morons' practical joke,
Aware of the threat in their whoops of delight
As their car roared off past a thirty sign.

I don't know what Plymouth is coming to –
It happened last week to a friend of mine –
The landlady said in the *Fortescue*,
As she kindly produced a warm damp cloth
To wipe the goo and bits of eggshell off.

GOLDFISH

I looked one morning and the lot had gone,
The dozen goldfish in my backyard pond;
The cull occurred one cold spell icy day.
It must have been the seagulls scoffed them all –
Were famished, probably, so *zap*. And *zap*.
The tabby cat from two doors down the street.
Who sometimes stalked the pond, was suspect, too,
Although I doubt he'd catch all twelve in one.
Odds on the seagull then. I'd plied the fish
With koi sticks daily (vitamin-enhanced),
And forked out fifty quid to pay for help
To change the water and clean out the pond –
Made out of fibreglass, ten foot by four.
Can't say I loved the fish, but did my bit;
They swam and jinked or hung about, gold-lithe,
Among the slimy lily stems and leaves.
I thought of films on Darwin on TV,
The struggle for existence and the rest,
How even in suburban Mannamead
It's dog eats dog in nature, so to speak:
A dozen goldfish down a gull's gullet.
I looked one morning and the lot had gone.

SORTING THE PAPERS OUT

Words of marital strife and hurt
In letters found by chance, and read,
Can't help but touch and disconcert,
Though those involved are all now dead.

High time to bin the letters, so
The pain at last is locked away
For good from sixty years ago?
I don't think kin should have to pay

Such bygone sorts of family debt.
Forbearance, then. Forgive. Forget.

BLACKTHORN

On some rough by the oil refinery
   Where the road bisects Ellesmere Port,
Through the car's nearside window my eye
   Was for a split second caught

By blackthorn out, in patches, silver-pale –
   Then a road-bridge, GUINNESS – and gone.
So with thoughts dead-set on their short-term goal
   (The journey, foot down, get on),

Delight, when it stirred, came nagged, as it were,
   By a kind of pulled tendon hurt;
The not having bothered that much this year,
   The not having stayed alert.

PLYMOUTH VIGNETTE

You can see 'Beryl Cook moments' everywhere
– Jess Wilder

In memory of Beryl Cook

The Dial-a-Dog-Wash van's appeared,
   With loads of dog-wash stuff on board,
To strike in our suburban street
   A likeably absurdist chord.

With k-swiss trainers on her feet,
   The dog-wash girl pads up the path
To sort the pooch at number eight.
   Shampooing? Grooming? Hydro-bath?

In Mutley Plain a pincher's booked
   To have its ID Microchip
And up Eggbuckland way a peke
   Is due for Flea Rinse and a Clip.

She's got a busy schedule, then;
   A sly half-smile plays on her lips;
Her white snug-fitting jeans reveal
   A plump backside and curvy hips –

At ease in big pink trainers, look,
A figure out of Beryl Cook.

DORCHESTER RURAL

Bridleway and beech-trees,
With robin-song and rook,
And sloes and old man's beard
In hedgerows, too – but look:

Below the wooden footbridge,
Front bumper in the stream,
A burnt-out joyride Peugeot
Mucks up both mood and theme;

In Indian summer sun,
Faint skeins of cirrus high,
The hatchback dumped and torched –
For heaven's sake, just why?

Schadenfreude impulse?
Binge drinking dare? Or joke?
Excess testosterone?
Amphetamines or coke?

Twenty thousand poundsworth
Of high spec tech gone west;
So much for Barnes's Dorset,
And all the rural rest.

SIGNS

The brand new industrial units
at the side of the M61
with steel cladding panels all painted
postmodernist dove-grey and plum,

are showing the effects already
of weathering's wear and tear;
a mould of moss by a down-spout,
and fresh rust-streaks here and there.

There's a notice on some of them, too,
To Let with Vacant Possession;
state of the art, the premises,
state of the world, recession.

For those with an eye for such things
(and a summary way with rhymes),
a townscape to note as symbolic.
an ironical sign of the times –

except that I think of John Galvin,
my friend, and of Mary, his wife;
John who built his building firm up
throughout the best years of his life,

till interest rates went through the roof,
and investment dropped through the floor,
so that client and subcontractor
couldn't meet their bills any more.

So when the bank refused him a loan,
the poor fellow went under and all,
and ironic's not quite the right term
for a friend gone like that to the wall.

While those with an eye for such things
may read subtexts in townscape, and spiel,
they remind me too much of my friend,
and what he and his missus must feel;

of how signs are just signs in the end,
at a zillion removes from the real.

G.W.

I hated you at first; slowly
Ploughing through a thick *Selborne*
One stuffy April in the library,
Five dilatory pages an afternoon,

Split up by coffee breaks hour long,
While thoughts in poker game got spent
To stave off reading further on
About just where ring ouzels went

In spring, how swallows' nests were built;
(Oozal or owsal, quipped my pen,
Among notes accreting slow as silt);
The whitethroat, chiffchaff, willow-wren —

So dottle-dry, compared to dice!

But things I came to prize, in time;
To see in shadows, bright as lace,
The crowfoot star a Berkshire stream,

Or the blue gleam of a damselfly
By flooded oyster beds one May,
Where curlews haunt with keening cry,
Or, surprised, catapult away,

Wings frantic, necks outstretched in fear.
Across the ebbing estuary.

Perceptions teenage crude, these fade
Compared to your keen eye, sixth sense,
Which sparked them, secretly. You made
Your village compass rich as France.

AFTERMATH

A new day followed, coldly, on
Our grief-day's burial adieus –
With Robin in the steading yard
Out working with his blackface ewes,
Robustly, by the dip's green slosh,
Dunking the creatures, one by one.
Though yesterday was obsequies,
Today is jobs that must be done.

HOPKINS AT ST BEUNO'S

'Enough for a patch on a Dutchman's trousers',
You remark of the clouds' small skylight of blue,
As, shying away from expecting too much,
We gaze from St Beuno's at Hopkins's view;

And then spot a kestrel, windhovering high –
The chance like some grace note of natural life
To claim as good fortune in a perspective
We share, I don't doubt, with the world and its wife.

Distrusting transcendence, all Hopkins perceived
Of Unity, Being and Creation *per se,*
Don't we sell his belief and his vision short
In our sceptical, twentieth century way?

The miracles, too, at St Winefride's Well
(Where Catholic and recusant pilgrims have come
To celebrate Mass, or to bathe and be healed,
Continuously over a millennium)

That led him to write of the spring water's 'stress',
As it brimmed and reflected God-given skies;
The Well was no grace note but manifest sign
Of imminent, unfailing Grace to his eyes.

And we know off by heart so much that he wrote,
For all it subverts our refractory view;
A hawk which we happened to spot, then was gone,
And the clouds' coincident patch of pure blue.

LEAVING TOWCESTER VICARAGE

Up and down the stairs, with clump of boot on board,
  The Pickfords men moved items, one by one;
    We talked of football with them over tea –
  The Hesketh bike, and what the Council'd done
    About its car-park scheme – phlegmatically,
      As if nothing untoward;
  Sat round the table this time, though, we knew
    Beyond the door there, in the stone-flagged hall,
    The books had gone, no Cruikshank on the wall …
The Cobblers start next season up at Crewe.

Keep busy now, and don't give in to gloom;
  I take my matches out, and then crouch down
    To set alight the mildewed leather box
  Of juvenilia I've dumped on the brown
    Dry earth, where iceberg roses and mauve phlox,
      Serene as ever, bloom.
  Then the acrid blue smoke-ribbons rise;
    While cool Madonna lilies in their row
    Next to the limestone wall, as ever, glow,
A past's detritus disperses to the skies.

The town-hall chimes, the church bell just behind,
  The 'synagogue' you won't lock any more.
    Its tolls, its quarter-peals, the eight o'clock,
  And big Vic Burt who rang them, strict as law,
    Blacksmith and verger, gone. How much comes back,
      Bewildering, to mind!
  Old Cyril Buckland's hand-cranked roundabout
    One damp June garden fete I helped to run;
    His wedding, with white horses and a brougham!
Like me, he's balding now, and getting stout.

Foxed pages of old registers recall
  The seventeenth century names we know –
    Dunkley, Loveridge, Allen and Linnell,
Father to son to son, unfolding slow
    Succession in the town, soul after soul,
      Each individual;
The parsons' scripts mark, birth by birth, each name,
  Yet telescoped as in a wink of time;
    Revs Lockwood, Roper, Ford, now you. That chime's
Rung out each day, three centuries, the same.

How we would listen to Mum's Delius,
  Together on the drawing-room settee,
    Two teenage boarding schoolboys there, all ears!
Like yesterday, it all comes back to me,
    Though you've not sat to play in recent years –
      That's what arthritis does.
And beds undug, well, what's the point, you say,
  We're off, we've grubbed up roots and bulbs to take
  For the 'box' we've bought – then, quietly, make
Your joke, it's a box we end up in, anyway.

Things helped to mar the last few months we had;
  Those plans to sell the house – *as offices!*
    They thought, the Goths, they'd get a new one built;
And sited in the garden, if you please!
    That Canon Urquart in it to the hilt;
      A stinker, and quite mad.
The PCC, thanks goodness, threw it out –
  The church is stuffed with bland committee men,
  Who'd join the Baptists, outlaw Series One;
None of them's an earthly what it's all about.

And one last time I wander round the side
　Along the passage we shot airguns in
　　To have a pee (old force of habit still)
　By outhouse fete flags, folding chairs, the bin,
　　Then leave, no looking back, by strength of will
　　　To shrug off what has died.
　And pegs still on the line – so normal, all –
　　Under the beech whose grape-dark August leaf
　　Lent relish to the heart yet, crossed by grief;
　Short tenancy of richness; leaves must fall.

I called in at Cold Higham afterward,
　Where my nephew and my niece were staying,
　　She engrossed in the *Boy Friend's* film remake
　He with a frisbee in the garden playing.
　　We spoke of school, swapped jokes, I tried to shake
　　　Dismay off – word by word.
　I'll not scythe nettles down again below
　　The apple-tree tangle, or feast my eye
　　On our yew and copper-beech. And so, goodbye.
　Soon on that bonfire ash, new grass will grow.

CONTINUUM

The 'Devil Among the Tailors'; the old folk tune,
Which a fiddler, busking, played
In Stockport's Merseyway, near Asda and Monsoon,
Echoed through the mall's postmodern glass arcade.

I recognised the air, reminded, like some cue,
How back in the eighteen-forties,
The tune was a favourite in Hardy's Dorset, too –
Or so he commented in one of his stories –

Not that the young Stockport fiddler would have known,
As he busked there in the mall,
Bowing away, engrossed, impromptu, on his own,
For the drive of the tune, lift of it all.

Line 8, in 'Absent-mindedness in a Church Choir'.

Reading a River (2005)

BOUNDARY LANE

Where Boundary Lane skirts high-rise Hulme,
What looks at first a fly-tip site –
Old bricks, ground elder and drab grass –
Has bluebells, too; its yeast of bloom.
One consequence of planning blight.

And in its inner city lung
Behind the Dar-ul-Amaan Club
And Lee's Kebab and Chicken place
Some goldfinches are scavenging
For thistle-seed among the scrub.

For all its wear, its traffic-fumes,
This frayed and dingy habitat
Deserves its due, distinctive gloss:
A *charm* of goldfinches. And Hulme's.
An offchance worth no less than that.

WHY CLIMB A MOUNTAIN?

Increasingly skew-whiff with each returning year,
the apple-tree boughs grope upwards, grow and sprout
southwards and eastwards out
in order to evade
to north and west the Goliath of a lime's
thick life-denying shade.

Crabwise, inch by inch, the Bramley climbs
its invisible cliff-face crag of light and air.
My tree, slow mountaineer,
goes on, because it's there.

READING A RIVER

A heron lifts away as we approach
Where cloud-grey Hodder and grey Ribble meet;
A spit of stones, an eddy-knuckled reach,
And glassy patch downstream as dark as peat.

There's movement in that pool, see? and you're sure
It's grayling, moving gently to large duns,
The Hodder, there, is acid, from the moor;
That's why it's good for autumn sea-trout runs.

What strikes my eye as surface, April-cool,
You read like braille, uncannily and clear,
Connecting signs of life in flow or pool;
A river's script, and palaeographer.

All waters have their temper, temperament,
Each river-face, its moods and tics and traits,
As individual as a finger-print;
The shoals and shallows, lies below still glaze,

And alders, stoneflies, sedges, each month's hatch
On Coquet, Lathkill, Driffield Beck or Dee;
A living web, I'd say, where you're in touch …
It's practice, pal, not flaming ESP;

It's try and try, a knack you pick up, right?
And 'knack' for 'art', you speak the northern way,
To deprecate what works like second sight,
Transforming all I saw that cloud-dulled day.

TURK'S HEAD

A beer-gut, bald, and fifty if a day,
He piped old airs, their lilt as good as new,
The Crooked Bawbee first, then *Rothbury Hills*;
Our ring of listeners gathered round and grew –

That pick-up band about him handing on
The tunes across the years, each jig, each dance,
Music that fathers and forefathers played
To young and old as now, no difference.

A lath-lean fiddler, long-nosed girl on flute,
Like faces from a print: *The Fete, Kermesse.*
You joined or left as freely as you liked.
This fete is all fetes in its timelessness:

A noon-time damp-charged sky, a small pub yard,
And *The Carrick Hornpipe* then *Sweet Hesleyside.*

WISH YOU WERE HERE

I tramped alone past limestone chine and bluff,
Up from the wind-vexed sea loch and *machair*.
Heather browned far moorland, curlews cried above,
In trackless leagues I longed that you could share.

With rod and bag I reached the white hotel –
My annexe room, its fifties' furniture;
But missing you, as dark on Fashven fell,
I went to join the anglers in the bar.

The Tweed, the Torridge; grilse and gillaroo;
Tackle, sea-trout, char; days in the rain and sun …
I missed you, yes; with whisky, though, wit grew,
As night-cap followed night-cap, one by one.

So ache of absence eased and, truth to tell,
I sloped off happy, love, to bed; slept well.

JOHN GLOVER

You'd rich success; were called the "English Claude";
Whatever, then, John Glover, made you sail,
An emigrant to far Van Dieman's land –
The Southern Cross above *its* Patterdale?

You'd wealth and, yes, a somewhat laughed-at fame,
An expert at Sublime and Pituresque;
But sold your seat up in the English Lakes
To settle near that quite unenglish Esk.

Did you with sure self-knowledge understand
Your life's work was small beer (each hackneyed view),
But in your bones could also sense you might,
At sixty-three, make up some sort of hand
From Bush and gum and glaring southern light –
Grandfather eyes turned young again, and true?

LCM OR HCF?

Dusty bay at a B-road's edge;
A gate-gap in what's left of hedge.
As I pull in for sun, pipe, view,
A wren lets rip with wrensong, too.

Though quite banal as moment-yield,
Both bird and rough ragworty field
Square perfectly with my *ad hoc*
Middle-of-nowhere dog days stop.

And strange how breaks like this possess
One factor, *sui generis*:
The way dull lay-bys, God knows why.
(Not being Lulworth Cove, Versailles,
Cape Wrath, Dove Cottage or Loch Ness)
Will etch their lines on consciousness.

FITZROY

Calm, like a hands-laid-on, as first light breaks
on the paperbarks' silver-grey frieze,
and a bronzewing flutes his three-note call
across the still creek and trees.

Then a tent-peg clinks, and somebody swears
as they fumble their tent-flap zip;
why shrug, why turn with such chagrin back
to friends, words, fellowship?

IVANHOE, NSW

Unchecked coarse grass, dock and clover
sprout between flags of the swimming-pool steps,
well on their way to greening them over;

there's a bench, upturned, by the pool inside,
while gum-nuts litter dry earth underneath
the deserted playground's swing and slide.

The chanced-upon settlement, sculpture-still,
lies, as if stunned, in the outback glare,
and so eerily silent it seems surreal,

where the only life in the brick-kiln heat –
baking each iron-roofed home in its plot
behind dusty trees in the empty street

as we stretch out limbs and fidget round –
are the irresolute shadow-pools we cast
on the washed-out khaki-coloured ground;

while, scuffed by some wind's breath off the plain,
a sand-plume unfurls in slow motion, like smoke,
to hover, half-billow, then subside again

to the press of heat and the sun-bruised still –
with a sort of shrug at its own lack of will.

LLANDUDNO SEASCAPE, WITH FIGURES

A pewter sea. No fishing smacks or sails.
A seafront palm, dishevelled by March gales.

And framed by wintry skies and low-tide sand,
In overcoats, two grey-haired women stand,

Braving the cold for snapshots on the prom –
One coat Saxe-blue, and one geranium.

Blue holds her brolly up (my, how it blows!)
With arm outstretched, mock Mary Poppins pose,

Then (look you) does a skittish schoolgirl skip
Of unexpected sprightliness, and *click*,

The moment's caught, plus pier and Orme and sea,
Dim Parcio and all. They laugh. Now tea.

Burlesque hit off with unselfconscious ease –
Two sisters – spinsters – lovers – divorcees? –

Without whom I should never have believed
How empty seascapes are when unrelieved.

Dim Parcio, No parking, in Welsh.

IN DUNHAM MASSEY PARK

In black leather jacket and pale blue jeans,
    On her own, unconcerned, in half-sun,
She was walking the broad grassed deer-park ride –
    As a man on his own might have done.

I'd like it, in fact, in Britain today,
    To be perfectly usual to see
What's not so usual – a woman, alone,
    Out walking as she was, and free,

Since that's what she'd simply chosen to do,
    Whether light-hearted or out of sorts,
For the fun or relief of it, solo,
    With her shadow, her dog or her thoughts.

It's not I've some project or programme
    Or social science theory to voice;
Just a yen or a wish that, as men have,
    Women had the scope of that choice –

To go for a tramp and be by themselves,
    Among oaks and head bare to the breeze,
Unanxious, unharassed, quite unremarked,
    And equal and really at ease.

JOHN SELL COTMAN AT ROKEBY

If faith can move mountains, so then can art –
As in Cotman's two *Views* of Greta Bridge:
The first features sky while the second depicts
A rugged and blue-shadowed fellside ridge.

All art is selection, as Cotman knew well,
At work on each similar, different scene,
With bogus blue hills for harmony's sake
Or counterfeit sky where hills should have been.

Almighty cheek or rank inconsistency
Or just artist's licence? The verdict depends
On *mimesis*, of course; how far can you go
Shunting landscape round as a means to your ends?

What magical weeks, though; Cotman at Rokeby;
What freshness and rightness of touch and of eye;
When 'ficle Dame Nature' was changed and improved
(Her sky turned to fellside, fellside to sky),

Was it faith of a kind, since a spirit had moved?

KIRKHOUSE

The whinstone sheepfold's been submerged by spruce,
Now they've put Kirkhouse Moor to commercial use;

And in thirty years they'll pick up a return
On their plantation leagues by Paddock Burn,

When the spruce is felled, once fully black and grown –
The sheep fold long since gone to heaps of stone.

Accountants costed what their Board would gross:
The trees their profit – and the moor our loss.

So spruce rows and gouged ditches, straight as dies,
Stain and deform each hill. It's enterprise.

That change is certain, is a truth as old
As truths the sheepfold stood for, and now sold.

MY TURN

My turn? OK. I throw the dice, get ten,
Glance down to see where boot is on the board,
Then count the squares from Pentonville and land
Slap bang on Vine Street with hotel. Oh *Lord*.

The children burst out laughing, since I'm sunk.
I groan, recount the squares – and play my role,
Knelt round the board with them (and largish scotch),
The grown-up stooge, good loser, life and soul.

I jolly through and trust, Dad, you'd approve
How I, though not as skilled as you were, play –
You gone, your role passed on – and can't but think
Again of you this Borders Hogmanay.
(A thousand quid? It can't be. Where's my drink ..?)
The Lord who gave; the Lord who takes away.

GLIMPSE

Below Wylam bridge, alone and absorbed,
An angler casts out. The spring salmon run;
Like new-minted silver, a dazzle downstream,
The Tyne's cold grey glaze transformed by March sun.

Dark shape against shine, in waders he stands,
Where I'd rather be, not car-bound *en route*
For Consett's Dipton crematorium –
In funeral temper, tie and best suit.

No chance, as I pass, of more than a glimpse,
Eyes skinned not for fish but the Whickham signs;
No chance of even the briefest of stops;
Great day, alright; lucky devil; tight lines …

You lived nearby, and surely would have known
The glimpse, my sense of seize the day and live –
The silvered Tyne, the salmon coming home –
Would understand, lost friend, and would forgive?

PUB LUNCH

"No chips for me", I fussed when you asked,
"I'm keeping an eye on my weight":
 Aware, as soon as the words were out,
 I'd said the wrong thing, but too late.

You had to build your body-weight up –
 So the consultant counselled you;
 Though as you couldn't digest solid food,
 It wasn't all that easy to do.

Yet in good part, as always of old,
 You were quick to relish the joke
 (Brother not putting his brain in gear
 As per usual before he spoke) –

 In the canalside pub at Stoke Bruerne,
 As bright, slow narrowboats passed,
 And August sun and your birthday, too,
 Which we couldn't but know was the last.

WOODBRIDGE

I glimpsed, from the hired limousine,
two boys, well-scarved against the sleet,

Each with a bright blue sledge, engrossed,
Setting out up the whitened street –

Like you and I, in Lancashire snow,
Long since, not a care in the world.

One hour afterwards, round your grave,
In bitter cold, snow-eddies swirled.

IN MEMORIAM A.M. 1948-1995

As kids traipsed off, in twos and threes,
    To school past pub, past betting-shop,
The sun lit up a crimson blaze
    In kerbside thorn-trees on Moor Top.
My post had brought a hoped-for cheque –
    A friend in France had sent a card –
A day that could have been designed
    To lull and catch one off one's guard.

At nine the phone went, and I heard.
    A heart-attack. At work. You'd died.
I stood there, speechless, while the sun
    Streamed on, mechanically, outside.
Mechanically, it must have lit
    Your Borders valley – Dod Hill Wood,
Lee Pen and white-harled kirk and house;
    Lit shock, lit loss, lit widowhood.

Just two short months ago, I stayed;
    A week when, why, we'd time to spare;
We beat the boys at badminton;
    Heard Brahms quartets down at Traquair;
The inn at Tweedsmuir, where we talked
    Of Heath Care Trusts – your work in Fife:
Your team, new colleagues, clinics, plans –
    A twinkle in your eye. New life.

I've snapshots of our long, last hike –
    The heather coming into flower;
Straw-hat and cod Edwardian pose,
    You stand, relaxed, by Blackhouse Tower.
The thistledown on Fethan Hill;
    Curlews above Mountbengerlaw;
The five of us at Tibbie Shiels –
    It seemed such times were all *encore*.

That phone-call morning when I learned
 In brute fact there'd be no again,
The sun streamed through my window-bay;
 A torpid wasp banged at a pane.
"We'll meet at Hogmanay," you wrote
 Three weeks ago, and sent a book
On Scott you'd seen and thought I'd like...
 Why, there you are by Blackhouse, look.

To try to comprehend, I read
 Donne's famous sermon; *Rasselas*;
Ecclesiastes; *Book of Prayer*;
 Of how man's life is but as grass...
Yet Sid Scam thrives; Stu Snout-in-Trough;
 Fritz Fraud; Hugh Huckster; and Sam Spiv,
While you, most generous of hosts,
 Had so much yet to do, and give.

To try to comprehend, I write
 Of valley, glebe and burnside trees,
The manse you made (in Hardy's phrase)
 A house of hospitalities –
To build a bridge across the void.
 Words make no sense. What can one say?
We thought we'd time; but we were wrong.
 We will not meet at Hogmanay.

Mechanically, the sun streams down
 On suburb street and shops, the same;
The kids traipse off to school once more;
 The leafless thorns no longer flame.
Mechanically, a curlew calls
 From Dod Hill Wood to Kirkhouse clear;
Hard by glebe-field and Quair, good friend,
 You lie, now, and you cannot hear.

IN MEMORY OF BILL RUDDICK

That time we took the Rydal 'upper path'
    To go to Mattins down in Grasmere church;
        That time on Dodd – wet-through from Lakeland rain;
Tarn Hows, that time, in deep snow one late March –
    I see you gesture, hear your voice again,
        As now the aftermath
Of recollection grows; those good days, gone.
    Faces and scenes from twenty years come back;
        'Viewing' Aira Force; Mirehouse walks; Tarn Beck;
The *George* at Keswick or the Grasmere *Swan* –

Where you'd talk on of southey, of 'Lodore';
    Of Rugby's Thomas Arnold at Fox How,
        ('Mere mountain and lake hunting is time lost');
The Wordsworths' early days at Windybrow;
    Dove Cottage, too, and Coleridge as guest –
        I hear your voice once more,
Then see you sat, unwell, two years ago,
    By Bassenthwaite and silhouetted fells
        You knew and loved – Barf, Causey Pike, Catbells –
The last time we were there; last cameo.

Fleas in the beds at Wythburn when Keats stayed –
    The funny side of things delighted you;
        The 'wretched' Liverpudlian called Crump
Who, building Allan Bank, wrecked Wordworth's view,
    And put him in the most almighty grump;
        The poem to a spade...
The flow of anecdotes stream back, pell-mell;
    How Wilkie Collins was laid up, quite lame,
        When he and Dickens (of all people) came:
He'd sprained his ankle up on Carrock Fell.

The jokes went with old-fashioned scholar skills,
   Though "suits", the "men in suits", now call the tune;
      What's "relevant"? What's "new"? But not, what's true? –
Helm Crag in May, beneath a crescent moon;
    The lovely *Grasmere* Farington once drew,
       Or *Skelwith Force*, by Hills.
Your learning, lightly worn, was shared, no side,
    So willingly with friends; one had a sense
    Of freedom from the grids relevance.
You were rereading Scott the week you died.

With "suits" now taking over literature,
   The Stokes-Nokes, Hobbs-Nobbs, Boot-Suit Theory type
      All fly their lightweight, opportunist kites,
As learning's lost in fashion and self-hype;
    Students are "customers"; quotations, "bites" –
      You found the "suits" a bore.
You'd deprecate the plaudit 'Humanist';
    In truth, Bill, it would well epitomise
    The 'spirit of Elian friendliness'
You lived for with such humour and such zest.

GLASS

A woman in a parka walks her dogs
On thin grass by the walled-up old wet dock;
From high-rise phosphate plant two men bike home
Along the towpath past pipeline and lock.

A ring of factories hems Spike Island in;
They're there because they're there, and must produce;
Detergents, pharmaceuticals and dyes
Sum fate up, here; fifteen decades of Use.

With haunts more like Giverny or Coole Park
Than grounds like these, leached out by *laissez-faire*,
Creative thoughts move in a higher class?

Yet workmen, woman, dogs; a gathering dark;
Flawed circumstance flawed Everyman must share –
So look, no condescension, in its glass?

TOWARDS FIDDLERS FERRY POWER STATION

A glaze of low-tide mudflats, Widnes marsh,
And in the air a sourish sulphur smell;
Spike Island's trees are saplings, scrub-growth young –
The green of reclamation, you can tell.

United Alkali's old Gossage works
Was flattened to the ground to make this park,
Grass acres ringed by new works' high tech steel,
Pale superstructures floodlit in half-dark.

A word like flange seems coined for such a place;
A chlorine, potash, soap and bleach town, right?
Its heritage is mass-productiveness.

Beyond the ground which grass and gorse renew,
The huge Rocksavage plant glows, light by light,
With turbines thrumming on, and work to do.

STANLOW

That something as utilitarian
As Stanlow's oil refinery at night
Should glow like distant, silver-pale *grisaille* –
Its fretted steel, a honeycomb of light…

Though functional as prose, there's beauty, too,
In how the floodlit complex strikes the eye;
Reactor vessels; high tech scrubbing towers;
A red flame burning waste off in black sky.

Vaccines to Weedol, bleach to PVC,
Commodities are what such plants produce;
And yet those lights, above the salt-marsh mist,
Create a sort of poetry from Use –
Subverting all we think that Art should be –
Organic in their way, and catalyst.

WIDNES: SPIKE ISLAND SPRING

The old dock mirrors thin all-over cloud –
The sun behind, pale as a watermark;
As blackbirds weave canalside lines of flight,
A couple walk the towpath through the park.

The blackbirds stake their territorial claims
On land with steam-wreathed cooling-towers above;
A line of factories rings the park's lung in,
Where lovers claim their time-off grounds of love

From work and nine-to-five, in weekend ease.
(One plant makes phosphates and another bleach,
Supply. Demand. Free Trade. Commodities).

Past anglers and the bearded boat-club man
They walk the springtime Sunday towpath reach.
You make of where you live the best you can.

SANKEY CANAL

A blackbird flits off low from towpath gorse
Across the silent, algae-choked canal –
So flat and still, it looks like pale green ice.
A tang of acid sours the salt-marsh chill.

As mudflat redshanks pipe thin counterpoint
To winds which fret old signal-box and shed,
All Sunday from the bleak grey phosphate plant
Steel flues spout steam and turbines pulse and thud.

The eye takes in this Widnes winter scene,
And spoil-heaps which rough grass and thorn renew,
The legacies of years of *laissez-faire*;

And then that boat, ablaze with Van Gogh blue –
Its cheerfulness so manic, it must mean
There's love behind its name, bright *Marie-Claire*.

CHEMICAL

The lung-corroding fumes; back-breaking toil;
The seething spoil-heaps of foul 'galligu';
The sting of chloride acid in the air;
The Mersey killed by toxin residue.

And yet (the 'yet' of Whig progressive views),
For all the cost, there were the benefits:
The medicines; the dyes; the bleach and soap.
The town improved, if once the very pits.

Were Muspratt, Gossage, Castner, Hutchinson,
Hard bastards or far-sighted pioneers?
Or was it mass-production's time had come,
Whose pawns they were as much as profiteers?

Some scars have healed, greened over, anyhow.
Their old wet dock's a lake with herons now.

QUINCE

The quince-tree's in leaf, and shadows the bay-window;
Two blackbirds skitter about
Above the first lilac and windblown red tulips
You say you can just make out.

You can see (more or less) how the ground at the back
Has begun to get overgrown;
But what can you do, with your legs so unsteady,
At ninety, and here on your own?

You peer at the garden, its brightness and shadow,
As springtime renews with a will.
Just the two of us now, who were four, left to hear
The quince-tree bird-song still.

BACK HOME...

However on earth can I tell you
The snowdrops you planted years since,
In their white and silent dozens,
Are in flower once again by the quince –
To distress you into recalling
The home we insisted you leave?
Is it best, then, not to tell you?
Or is not-to-distress to deceive?

WASPS IN THE HOME

In normal circumstances (which don't pertain),
We would without a doubt have taken
The set-back that morning in our stride
Which instead left you very much shaken.

They'd found a wasps' nest up in the eaves,
So indignant wasps were milling about
In the room next to yours. Staff had no choice
But there and then to move you out.

It's like bedlam, you said in your muddle,
And our outing got off to a bad start;
Unforecast rain then compounded ill-luck;
Enough to make anyone lose heart.

We've time though, surely, still, for second thoughts,
To make light of what happened, and agree
What a teacup storm those wasps really were.
Pretend things remain as they used to be.

BREEZY PRESTATYN

Having adjusted the flaps for your feet
    And tucked the rug in round your knees,
I wheel the wheelchair along sand-strewn flags
    On Prestatyn prom in the breeze –
Past a red-head out walking her collie,
    Two youths playing ducks and drakes,
A black-headed gull, clear-etched against blue,
    And breaker's spray-spout as it breaks.

Subjects which Hopkins, who knew this coast well,
    Would without much doubt have imbued,
Thanks to a gift one could call second sight,
    With a sense of infinitude;
Their instress divine and thus radiant,
    As earnest of God-ordained worth –
In contrast to which our presence must seem
    Unradiantly down-to-earth.

If we miss out on the uplift of instress,
    And sell the transcendent short,
This midday hour or so's change of scene
    Is much as we hoped for, and sought;
Where, for all that the prospect is finite,
    You may sit, rug warm round your knees,
Tired eyes drinking in whatever they can
    Of girl, wind-buoyed gull and Welsh seas.

SLOES

Three years ago, I took you in the car
To help with picking sloes to make sloe gin,
By Kingthorn Mill down on the Bradden lane.
It meant a change for you, was not that far,
And you could walk still, then, and so join in.

And now I've come in late September cool,
A hundred miles from Bradden and the mill,
To gather sloes once more, in Manchester,
A rec with traffic noise near Parrs Wood School;
The site has changed, but not the ritual.

Sleeves wringing wet from blackthorn drenched with rain,
I carry back perhaps two pounds of sloes –
Small change of news, as well, to share with you:
"Been busy, Mum! It's sloe gin time again",
Though in the Home you're yonderly, God knows,

In such a state how can you care that much,
For all I'll talk as if we're quite in touch?

WEYMOUTH NIGHTINGALE

As ring-road cars thwacked past the parking spot
Where kissing-gate gives on to reed-beds path,
I picked out, just, his rising, falling song
In air still damp from cloudburst aftermath.

The warden told me that I'd hear him there,
The nightingale, my May Day singleton,
Secure in fading light and roadside gorse,
His journey out of Africa now done.

Those haunting, half-heard notes were something, too,
That if you could, you would have loved to share,
Asleep now in the Home, ten miles away,
Your brain confounded by dementia;

A song which must, instead, suffice as news
To talk of when I come tomorrow night,
For all I'm doubtful if you'll take it in…
To think of journey's end, though; fading light;

And nightingales that once you told me of,
In Towcester churchyard, forty years ago –
So much floods back to mind, of worth, of loss,
Of time that's gone, and debt of thanks I owe.

COLLEAGUE

Our colleague, Ernest Young, expounds
    To first year 'kids' upon
Metadiegetic discourse
    In Dickens and in Donne.

He thinks he'll make a Chair before
    He's thirty-eight or so;
His latest work is due out soon
    On Methuen Video.

Archaic bourgeois structures must
    Dictate a bourgeois text:
That methodology once grasped,
    It's hermeneutics next.

He's a brand-new desk computer
    For poems he takes to bits.
'The author's dead', you understand;
    In his place our Ernest sits.

READER

"We've colleagues so crazed about *relevance*, now,
That they'll set strip cartoons as a classroom text.
Like a page of Jane Austen, is that what they mean?
It's such eyewash" she adds. "I ask you, what next?"

There in her bookcase, the Cadell Walter Scott.
"One gets, don't you know, so frightfully weary
Of all this infernal jargon and piejaw
Of -ology, -ism and theory of theory.

It's so utilitarian, and it deprives
The young of their rights to the classics the need..."
On the bureau below the 'Wordsworth' by Shuter
Lies her Blackwood's edition of *Adam Bede*.

SPORTS FIELD, SOUTH MANCHESTER

Hands numb, lungs rasping – about one tenth alive –
I whistle up. Touch-down? Knock-on? Scrum five?
Don't know. Don't care. The try line's lost in snow,
While the wind-chill factor chills like ten below.
My borrowed boots are pinching, and they hurt.
The sweat has turned to ice inside my shirt.

"Stamp your authority on the game, you're boss"
They said. But Lord, this is ridiculous;
It's *sleeting* now. Oh I'm an ace BF
For promising to come and effing ref.
What Paradise is like, though, I see clear:
A long, hot bath, a bar and lots of beer.

SLOTH

Sweet-talking, ever-present voice,
good friend and old familiar,
tyre round the midriff, treble-chinned,
long hopeful-travelling non-arriver –
though gross in size, you still retain
such silver-toned and subtle charm
that your tongue works like mandragora;

whose words (more sensitive-unerring than
the most ultrasonic microwave device)
will always home direct in on
that recess in our hearts
where deep complaisance lurks –
unswervingly, hypnotically;
wizard malingerer, loveable skrimshanker.

GERMAN LESSON: SUB-TEXT

She stands *behind* a chair *beside* the clock
Beneath the portrait *on* the mantelshelf.
It's Gertrud Muller, merchant Muller's wife;
"Herr Smith, now let me introduce myself".

How are you – very well – and did you take
The stopping train – oh yes, and then the bus,
Which left at half-past five (*halb sechs*, that is,
As Fraulein, with a halb-smile, says to us).

Herr Muller has a nose, two ears, dark hair,
A jacket and a tie, a brief-case, so,
But Fraulein, as you state this, *ironisch*,
There're other things we're bursting, like, to know:

Love-talk words, for instance – right pitch and right tone, too,
Oh let's doff grammar-clothes. Your eyes suggest it. Do.

CRITICAL REVIEW, OR DON'T FLY OFF THE HANDLE

From what he writes, you'd think the End was Nigh,
(I've known the feeling often, at Turf Moor:
The team quite *terrible*, the ref a fiend,
And three goals down, and Armageddon sure).

From what he writes, reviewing some poor sap,
You're put in mind of rape, or sacrilege;
Anathema and curse! How is it books
Provoke such high intensity of rage?

Forgo your verbal *Schadenfreude*, please,
Don't shoot the sap, he's done his level best;
Incongruous excess of phrase recalls
Don Quixote, Almaviva and the rest –
Those archetypes of all that's comic-sad...

Recalls, as well, the critics Mozart had.

IN THE WINDOW OF A CITY CENTRE ANTIQUE SHOP

The spotlight halo, soft as bloom,
    Commode, cheval-glass, secretaire;
"What lovely things!" you say; and sigh;
    For stuff like that works out so dear.

So *we* can't murmur, back at home,
    To guests, with ease, with airiness,
"So nice to have such *nice* things round!"
    Those emblems of good taste, success.

Our dull and rented furnishings
    In job lots, cheap, the landlord bought.
Must nice things one day witness how
    Love's grown to need their mute support.

YVOIRE

for the Withdick-Pates

Midnight, now, and not a soul
on terrace, seat or lawn;
the empty promenade is paved
by geometries of shadow, all's still,
the atmosphere like vacuum –
except for where
a cowl of motionless and swarthy pines
steep-hems the harbour, close,
and the port's eye, restless, glitters.
How muscular and coal-glaze waves
in its rock-dark cockpit swell,
each bulge and buckle, seesaw tilt and hump,
by star-reflections ridden –
slippery, split mercury.
How exhaustlessly, with glob and plock,
the water, nervy, slaps
the rib and keel
of twenty tethered yachts,
white-hulled, compact as shells
and as perfect in their shapes,
in line, there, at the groyne.
How brittle, tense and taut
like highly-strung and
tight-reined colts they strain.

And what an eerie dance of sound
the halyards and the rigging make
on high spar and on creaking mast,
with tap-tap fret and horse's bridle clink.

Paths and grass are hushed, all's absence there,
yet how the white yachts bob and toss
as in a weird infectious chafe of desire,
charging the midnight dark
with electricity of expectation.

ON THE ABTHORPE ROAD

'Cut vines and osier
Plash hedge of enclosure'
– Tusser Feby's Husbandrie, quoted in Thomas Sternberg's
The Dialect and Folklore of Northamptonshire

Tonsured trim as suburb box,
This hawthorn hedge, *en brosse,*
Invests the lane with change –
With city stylishness.

No need of men to plash
The upright hedge-stems, now,
To peg them, chopped and bent,
Above cleared ditches' brow

To familiar thick-set frame.
This tonsure shows us how things go.
The plashing of hawthorn here
Was a human craft, but slow.

Quick and cheap, the powered shears,
So farmers, accounting, can subtract
Hedge-setting from man-hours.
Neccessity's frame, in fact,

Confronts my weekender's eyes,
Who'd foist Arcadia where
Profit and loss oblige.
Most hedges began as Enclosure.

Across accountable land
A silo in sunlight glints neat.
'Silo' one's come to understand.
'Plash' will soon be obsolete.

GLOUCESTERSHIRE ALLIANCE, 1985

Reading the sports page through, I see
That Tewkesbury Rovers went two up
Last week, at Wick, through goals by Lea;
That Wilmcote won the John Wood Cup;

But Adlestrop – *they* crashed 4-1
At home to Chadlington, it seems,
Positioned here (some *cachet* gone)
Among the local soccer teams

Of Oxfordshire and Gloucestershire.
So evening *Stars* and *Mercuries*
Encompass matches everywhere
In small print mid-March summaries –

A bit like hawthorn hedged about
Rough pitches marked on rec and field
Year after year close-mapping out
Dense worlds of Trophy, Cup and Shield.

Near clinker lanes, allotment ends,
By pond and pylon, swing and slide,
Flower marginal and countless grounds
For fellowship, all England-wide,

Evoking countless memories
Now, as in twenty-, fifty-five,
Of shot, save, tackle, move and miss:
Quixotic, teeming, rich, alive.

Turf hushed tonight, in dark and dews,
Under perennial, damp-charged sky;
Where ghostly figures, stamping shoes,
Watch ghost-teams fight their needle tie.

THINKING OF MATTHEW ARNOLD ON THE M62

for Park and Jeannette Honan

"To see things as they really are", you wrote;
    But it was northern slum-schools you saw true,
        With Bradshaw's lines to con, not Greek, each day,
    Linking those factory towns you journeyed to.
        Amid such "grimness, bareness", then, what "stay" –
            From all you loved remote?
    Each night to lodgings you returned
        From days passed marking notes on algebra
        Or school-books ("dirty, ditto furniture");
    A poet into HMI transformed.

On one side, half-fed children, stunted growth,
    The working slums, girls in mills and mines;
        What could "ennoble" this, what "animate"?
    And then the middle class, your "Philistines",
        More passionate for railways than for "light" –
            And you estranged from both.
    What you saw truly, time and time again,
        Was something poetry could never feed,
        Nor urging dreams of Greece, and man's sore need
    For Homer, "simple, rapid, noble, plain".

You wrote your *Scholar Gypsy*, then, as well,
    Those timeless Berkshire fields a world away
        From schools in Blyth and York, reports to pore,
    Three hundred orals taken in one day,
        And pupil-teacher papers, by the score:
            The spiritual. The real.

Your scholar sought pure self, intuitive,
        Neglectful of career, the world of men;
        In what dour digs did you conceive, and when,
That symbol of free spirit, and that myth?

What of them now? Pure self, "ennoblement"?
        We've read so much; we're modern, knowing, wise.
            "His thin red line of verse, still holding out?"
        We joke of him, sat warm in Faculties,
            Distrusting dreams, ironical about
                His "touchstones"... tolerant.
        For fifty-one per cent can now afford
            Their central heat, and ninety have TV;
            O brave new liberal democracy,
        Where one in five now holidays abroad!

How out of date he feels! What dreams he had!
        I speed across the Pennines. I, too, teach.
            Lamplight and headlight shape things frosty-clear.
        We're turning Shakespeare into common speech,
            And Greek's been lost, the tongue he held so dear;
                It's how things go. Too bad.
        Great boards of blur and white unlyrically
            Highlight Leeds and Pontefract; snowflakes fall;
            Unfestal bulbs prink out a Bingo Hall;
        On a blankness of Clearway, trucks thwack by.

MARKET STREET

In a wash of autumn crowds, we stop to kiss goodbye;
    You've only just got time to buy some things for tea.
You're sorry, but there, you've a family to cook for;
        I'm so lucky, you add. I'm free.

We stop to kiss goodbye. Then I am free to go,
    With prospects wide as seas, yes, choice on every hand;
The town my oyster, each evening hour my own,
        And life my kingdom to command.

Dear, do you covet this, my range of liberty,
    Weighed down by shopping, in the store's slow queue?
If you could only sense how blank its compass seems
        As I walk up Market Street, away from you.

IN NOVEMBER

In November, when the elm has shed
Its yellowed leaves across the asphalt's grey,
And suburb gusts and traffic slipstreams sweep
Them under our parked cars,
Against the whitewashed stones,
In at the double-doors,
New vistas open up, of winter muddy skies;
In summer vision's circumscribed by green,
But now we see the single magpie come,
Flash of satin blue upon his side,
To trespass in the forecourt here.
Most days he comes, to make me wonder why
He sticks to these few outskirts acres, so;
Surmise he knows
He can scavenge in old safety here, heeds
By instinct sheer necessity. Which same force,
Perhaps, determines more than his winged life;
May drive, unconsciously,
Our morning faces out to shops
For bread each day; and tempt small cars with Ls
At snail's pace three-point turns and starts and stops
Year-round in neighbouring streets; and infiltrate
Buff envelopes demanding rates
Inside each house in spring; and make
The tinny bells of brick St Chad's
Chime Sunday services; and drain
Dull whiteness from the sky just now,
Hardening street-lamp ingots of fluorescent light
Against the gloom; and compel each twenty-two
Half-hourly past our stop,
From Urmston to Levenshulme, and back.

BLOOM

A stone's throw off from Brian's Grill, and where
I'd booked the joke, 'the backroom with a view'
(Wet yards, asbestos roofs, bike-wheel and weeds,
Some panes of cloud, and much like Stockport, too)
Lay Eccles Street and Bloom's; which was, I saw,
Good Georgian, derelict; for which, I know,
Developers have blueprints planned, like home,
For high-rise slabs; and like home, good will go.

From dives around Abbey Street pulsed sounds of rock,
Since Dublin's internationalist these days;
I traced Bloom's path, from pilgrim interest,
That Everyman whose thoughts still emblemize
A human scale – provincial, decent, deep –
Our noise-nagged, cash-crazed polities hold cheap.

IN MEMORY OF PATRICK KAVANAGH

By lower Baggot Street, I found your lock:
Near Maxol Car Wash and where office towered
On each hand high, your poem and your bench –
The Dublin air with traffic thick and soured.

It should have been so otherwise, not flawed;
The oil-brown water scummed; the dripping gate;
A plastic bag; grey spars of two-by-one.
That haunted place should be inviolate.

Such stony ground a let-down, I recalled
The sunset conjuring a mist of light
From mica-specks within the granite grain
Along Dun Laoghaire harbour's huge sea-wall,
As if brute rock bore life. The way the song
You conjured out of stoniness lives on.

HOME THOUGHTS FROM THE KIMBERLEYS, WA

Where corellas, disturbed,
set up their hoarse shriek
above paperbarks lining
this unearthly-still creek,

an escarpment cliff-face
millions of years old
burns in the sun-glare
dark-tawny, pale gold –

to remind me, bizarrely,
of the rust-coloured stone
of Northamptonshire farms
I know well from home.

Unlikeness and likeness:
how we crave to relate
to the utter remoteness
of time beyond date –

like readings my mind's eye
brings vainly to bear
on horizons in a heat-pall
harsh bird-screams tear.

Off dirt-tracks, odd homesteads
bear names, too, that tell
what haunted first settlers:
Glencoe, Lissadell.

SYDNEY BRICK

The city's rich with one Lancastrian thing –
And that's red-brick. The good-bad-poem sort:
Some looks like raw rump steak, some's lobsterish;
Some's rosé pale; some shines like ruby port.

Some's apoplectic mauve and cheek by jowl
With glazed red-brick with Kranski sausage hues;
A red mosaic sprawl across the hills
From Ryde to Marrickville to La Perouse;

Maroon or fiery or plain ruddy brown,
Each one's red-brick breams out its different glow
In Bronte, Abbotsford and Wollstonecraft,
From school, shop, duplex, block and bungalow;

With constant startle, eyesight almost aches,
As Sydney brick in Sydney sunshine bakes.

A JAR WITH GLEN FITZGERALD: EXPOSTULATION AND REPLY

The Brits are Poms, OK. But when I press,
The Scots, I find, and Welshmen, are alright.
Press further then. Northumbrian? Or Scouse?
Or Brummie, Geordie, Dorset, Isle of Wight?
Press Catholic Scots, press Presbyterian;
Press Lancs v Yorks, what Wearside thinks of Tyne;
What Cornishmen of Devon men will say –
We're Poms are we? Well, come on, Glen, *define*!
To blazes Men of Kent and Wiganers?
The devil take all Lincoln folk and Tykes?
To hell with, what, soft Pommie Bristol burr?
The cockney of Sam Weller or Bill Sikes?
O richer far than poverty of Pom,
Can't each on differ, as and where they're from?

Fitzgerald replies
What Pom means, mate, is things like Bodyline;
It's the hypocrisy that makes us sick;
The steel below the well-bred velvet voice;
The will to win by any lousy trick.

You coined the phrase Fair Play, the Game's the Thing,
The Amateur, Good Sport – fair dos, that's fine
(It's Taking Part and Not the Winning Counts...)
Then Poms invented bloody Bodyline.

PRAYER

St Christopher, protect us, please,
    From man with his Sony Walkman set,
Afraid of silence as of speech –
    Locked in his headphones' *oubliette*;

O comfort those compelled to hear
    His ceaseless double concerto tape
For bluebottle and squeaky chalk
    In train or bus, and no escape;

Look kindly on the traveller
    Condemned to eavesdrop group or band
Whose constant unoiled-wheel-cum-whizz
    Is more than flesh and blood can stand.

PICASSO, LATE DRAWINGS, AT GENEVA

Pornographie de vieillard!
Dieu te punira!

In the remarks' book at the Picasso show
The bold but childlike script condemns,
Condemns. Punish the old pornographer!
　　Sees breast, hair, buttocks, lip and limbs,

Refracted by loving, derided sense;
Ageless the lady: so alive and assured!
To the dance of desire, like a lap-dog,
　　Art's irrepressibly lured:

Where, as the dancer, it shines. And those prim words
Of jealous, self-righteous, primitive hate
Scald in the air-conditioning.
　　Who said that we'd progressed, of late?

PRODIGAL

It's hard, when you think of it, not to feel
Considerable sympathy lurk
For the parable prodigal's brother –
The one who got on with his work,

Husbanding cattle, tilling the fields,
And dependably helping his dad,
While his sibling waltzed off with the money,
Then careered downhill to the bad.

For all that you see the father's point
About the son lost and then found,
There's a case to make for the one who stayed put,
Industrious, loyal and sound.

No wonder he took his father to task –
What happened was more than enough:
The spendthrift returned; the fatted calf hoopla;
The music and dancing and stuff.

Salvation and Grace to all sinners
Is of course what the moral entails;
But why should thanksgiving so wholly involve
The brother who went off the rails?

Aren't the values of journeyman duty
Meet, too, to make merry, be glad,
As much as contrition and heartfelt remorse
From a penitent Jack the Lad?

To forgiving's disproportionate joy
One defers (*felix culpa*) – yet, Lord,
Must we accept that devoted long service
Should suffice as its own damned reward?

OH

Oh, to get poems
    back on the page –
not ode as performance
    or stanza on stage,
but print in a book
    with words we may hear
in solitude speak
    to the inner ear,
and which, when we choose,
    we may re-read
in the freedom of quiet –
    for inner need.

LETTERS

"Dear Johns", they are called –
    in effect, just as if
it is always the lady
    who ups and goes off;

yet the phrase, with its hint
    of Woman as Eve,
("walked out on her fellow,
    now would you believe?")

takes little account
    of that final "Dear Ann"
sent off by old Adam
    when *he* cut and ran.

CONTEXT, PROFILE, IMAGE, IMPACT, MISSION

Viewed in the Context of Profile and Image
  most managements now require,
we're not, as a big department goes, the sort
  "to set the Thames on fire";

a river which (think of it) burst into flame
  for sure would have Impact;
as Mission, though, what would the point be,
  viewed in a Context of fact?

BLURB

These poems are "sassy", says the blurb,
  To lead you to surmise
That knowingness spells knowledge now;
  Street wisdom equals wise.

ST OLAF'S, WASDALE HEAD

St Olaf's church at the dalehead stands
In peace beyond the gloomy Screes;
Where the vicar from 'forty to 'forty-one
Was the Reverend George O'Cheese.

THOMAS BEWICK

Your graver's tempered steel
 From dead grain yields its line;
 Fur-soft, smoke-lithe or exact
As a brim's stir in your Tyne.

You "stuck to nature closely",
 Despite laborious means,
 Cutting your peacock's fan –
Your drunk, who sees two moons –

Your unconventional,
 Unclassical thrush and lark;
"Beautiful aireal wanderers",
 Immediate and life-like.

And so – a temperate,
 God-fearing, dyed-in-the-wool,
 Individualistic,
 Northumbrian provincial –

You revived the lost skills
Of the craftsman-engraver;
Both deviser-designer
And populariser.

*

Can revolutionary art
 Have been ever so modest
 As yours, Thomas Bewick?
 Who in "kitchen work" traced

On blocks inches square
"Nature up to nature's God",
Creating an Empire from
One parish neighbourhood,

To establish the mystery
Of boxwood engraving –
That fine-as-leaf-vein craft,
Demotic, moral, loving.

WILLIAM PAYNE

In Plymouth City Gallery,
     One Christmas Eve, all rain,
I saw a retrospective
     Of painter "Payne's Grey" Payne,
Whose name will mean forever
     That earthy, darkish hue
He mixed from yellow ochre,
     Lake and Prussian blue.

More dense than Indian ink,
     Those Payne's grey washes made
The middle distance deeper,
     With shade that looked like shade,
In picturesque topography
     And local landscape view,
Like Mutton Cove or Pengersick,
     Or Stonehouse Hill or Looe.

From the swan baptised as Bewick's,
     Via Bank's Banksia rose
To Canon Greenwell's Glory,
     Payne stands foursquare with those
Whose names fused with the language
     And still survive today:
A waterfowl; a flower;
     A dry-fly – and a grey.

Eponymously genial,
     They were creators who
Descrived the nondescript,
     If small-scale, no less new;
Extending our awareness,
     Enriching the mundane –
Like a wet-through day enhanced
     Through meeting William Payne.

GOOD HUSBANDRY

Good husbandry: a phrase to hint at life
Whose ends cohere, in harmony with means;
Far-sighted; sane; frugal as coppicing,
One with the earth as each new season greens.

To what avail, such prescient foresight, when
Some highday binge, unbargained for, transpires –
Release from order, break-out from routine?
Drink deep for here and now; light roaring fires.

You can't but see how anarchy appeals,
Uplifted as you must be as you gaze,
For all its waste, its short-term, spendthrift spell:
A useless, consuming, magnificent blaze.

D.I.Y.

Out the gnarled bricks of the old fireplace come:
Down-to-basics world. Black-and-Decker-dom.
Mortar-clogged my nails, grime and soot in hair,
And rubble-dust's hoar-frost on shelf and chair,
I drill, then tap, then lever, coax – and *thump!*
The buggers crash in dirt-plumes, lump on lump.

And next by stages built up, bit by bit,
Clean lengths of timber in the gape's gap fit.
A joist's cemented in to hold the weight;
An upright braced; a chamfer chiselled straight;
The saw is urged through softwood 2 x 2;
Then mouldings mitred, millimetre true.

Framework to finish, the firm structure grows;
From mind and muscle matched, enjoyment flows.
At length there's plastering, to plumb-line cord,
Undercoat and topcoat, smooth as a board –
Sponged flush, dried out, and sanded well when set,
Then painted thrice… This world's compact. Complete.

Compared to such plain work, poems seem unreal.
That architrave, that surface, now: just *feel!*
Yet soon to worlds less sure, the mind returns;
Lamplight on papers in a far room burns.
So dusty, tingling, tired – achievement-dry –
My hand takes up the pen. But doubtfully.

LANE

Upgrading once decided on,
the County Council set about
this Heart of England grass-verged lane
which goes from Litchborough to Duncote,
cementing kerbstones at each edge.
Now in the April evening light,
instead of ditch and hawthorn hedge,
your eye is held by a die-straight white
perspective of official kerb;

more country gone for more suburb.

ON THE ROAD

Low sun from Bradden way reflects
a paleness like hoar-frost
off moisture left on winter wheat
by vanished early mist;

where all is still, save kneading swarms
of mote-sized morning midges,
hovering just above the mud
of tyre-stamped road-side ridges;

whose hour-long insect lives must have
their due purpose, I daresay,
in a general scheme of things,
and part or bit-part to play –

yet perturb the outward stillness
and answering inner peace,
and whether we like it or no
cannot and will not cease.

ENVOI

Hadyn/Hofstetter (?) String Quartet Op 3 No 5

for Paddy and Nina Stephenson

We may never know for sure
Who wrote that haunting serenade;
But as Haydn has so much more,
Let Hofstetter not be denied –
So he may shine, a minor star,
In excellence a singleton,
Like Eichner, Litolf and such men
Whom genius touched, it seems, by chance,
Just once.